NOSTRILS TO ENLIGHTENMENT

Gary Nostrils

Copyright © 2019 Timothy Monley
All rights reserved.
ISBN: 978-0-6485371-1-3

To all the nostrils of the world

Your True Purpose

The true purpose of life is right in front of you. It has been there all along.

The secret of all wisdom is hidden right in front of you. Right in the middle of your face. The answer to all your questions is in your nostrils.

Do not be distracted by the head, the heart, the genitals, no other body part can give you the wisdom you seek. Only the nose in its humble glory can reveal the secrets of the universe.

Delve into the darkness of your nostrils and from them will emanate the light of consciousness.

Your Spiritual Journey

The fact you were drawn to this book is not coincidence, your nose has smelled this book from afar and drawn you here. You are ready to open your nostrils to the truth and begin a spiritual journey.

Your journey doesn't begin with a step of your feet, it begins with a flare of your nostrils. A widening of your opening to the truth.

Your road of truth will be your breath and your feet will be your nostrils. You will step far on them, but you won't need boots, little nose boots, on little nostril feet. No, just a willingness to open your nostrils to the wisdom in the air around you.

Does my nose need a guru?

Yes, and no. You do not need a person who calls themselves a guru, but your nostrils must find guru nostrils.

I was lucky enough to have two flies with enlightened nostrils fly into my nose to give me their wisdom, but we can't all stand around in paddocks waiting for enlightened flies like I did.

You must learn the art of nostril yoga and receive enlightened breath. The guru nostrils will breath in the out breath of the disciple, purify them and breath them back into the humble and devoted nose.

Through this process the pilgrim nostrils make their way closer to their divine nature.

Nostril Yoga

It is important to widen the nostrils as much as possible in order to increase your chance of breathing in enlightenment. With practice you will be able to increase the flare of your nostrils purely with your enlightened will. But at first it may be necessary to use your fingers to push your nostrils out.

Practice regularly and eventually your nostrils will become supple and expansive, ready to be gracefully penetrated by the air of enlightenment.

As you breathe with wide open nostrils you may start to feel a bit light and dizzy, that is great, that means you are beginning to receive the breath of enlightenment. It has absolutely nothing to do with hyperventilating.

Enlightened Nostril Super Powers?

It can be tempting to contemplate nostril widening surgery to rapidly increase your potential for enlightened breath. This new phenomenon may one day lead to a race of super nostril humans with extraordinary abilities. However, suddenly acquiring a large pair of nostrils could lead to you inhaling more negativity as well as more enlightenment and that could make your nose explode.

It is important to practice daily and gradually increase your nostril power. With time and diligence, you may well become part of a race of super nostril beings, capable of levitating cats and using their nostrils as a torch at night.

Nostrils and Love

To widen the nostrils is to widen love. The expansion of the nose frees the heart, making you more able to connect to others and experience fulfilling relationships. As you learn to widen your nostrils people will naturally become more attracted to you.

By practicing nostril yoga while on a date you can greatly increase your chances of finding a soul mate. Get as close as possible to them and flare your nostrils as wide as possible, your nose will be communicating directly with theirs and will form a spiritual connection. As your nostrils express their desire to breathe each other you will be drawn together and loving good times will begin.

Nostril Self Defense

If you find yourself in a negative energy situation it might be necessary to breathe entirely through your mouth. This defensive breath will protect you from absorbing any ignorance or negativity from the air around you. Open your mouth very wide and breathe very shallowly to dissipate the unenlightened air. Your eyes can also help you to deflect the negative energy. Open them as wide as possible and look direct at the source of negativity. By refusing to absorb their negativity in this they will most likely be confused. It is also possible the negativity will remain in their presence and they might get more angry, if this happens it is advisable to run away.

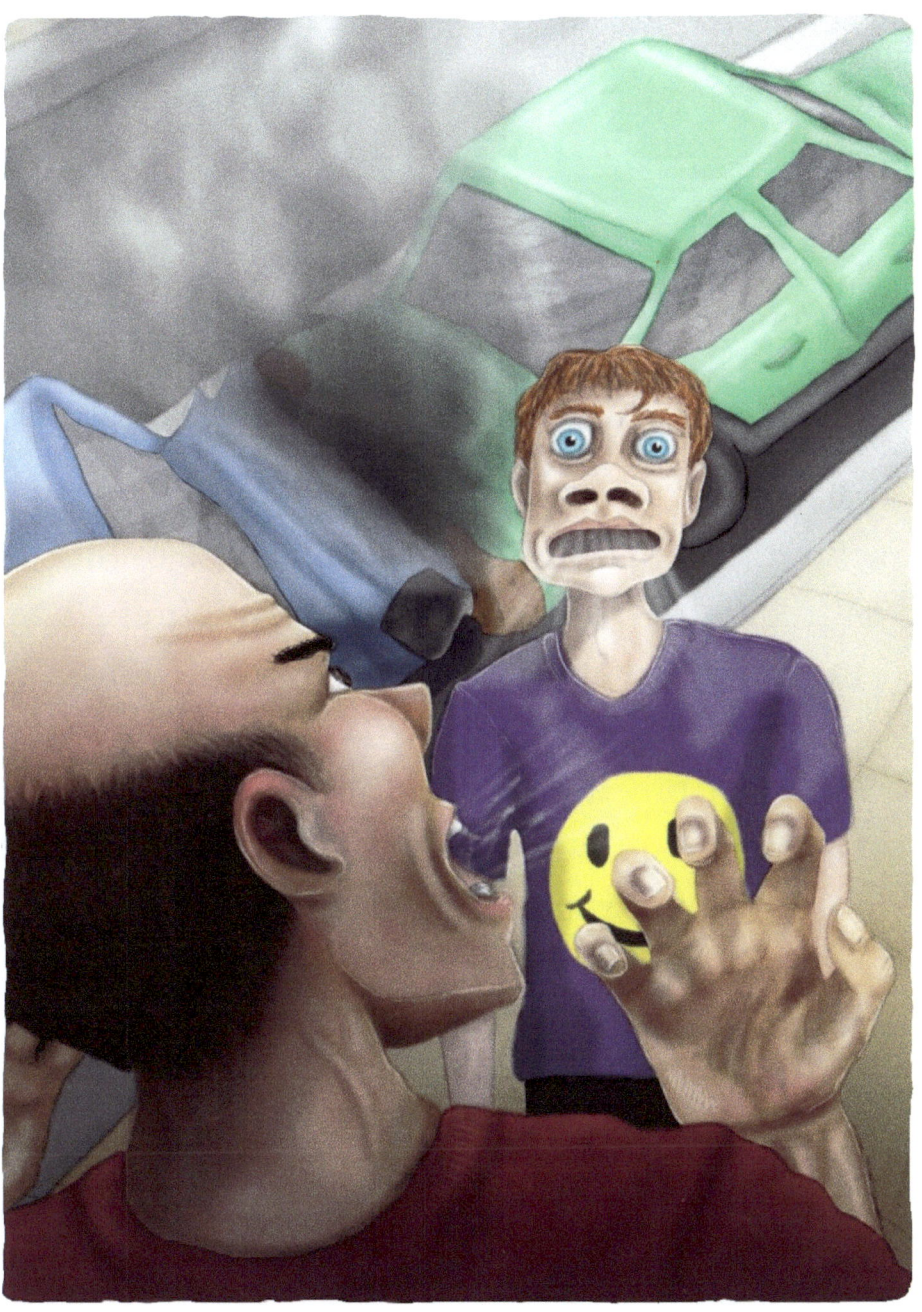

Nostril Soul Cleanse

As you widen your nostrils you will start to clear out all the negativity in your body. During this process it is important to not shower in anything other than pure spring water and not to use any soaps or perfumes. Soap is a lie we use to hide the truth of who we are. To become enlightened, you must adopt an attitude of extreme smell honesty.

As you practice nostril yoga and release yourself from the illusion of artificial fragrance your body will begin to reveal its smell truth or Smuth. This Smuth may be quite ripe to begin with and you will need to begin cleansing you scent chakras.

The Six Scent Chakras

There are six scents chakras on the body which must be cleansed regularly to maintain your smell health, or smelth. As you break free from the lies of soap you will be able to assess your smuth and start to heal your smelth.

In order to cleanse your scent chakras must get your nose as close as possible to them, ideally gently touching them with the soft tip of your nose. Widen your nostrils and breathe steadily and deeply. The stronger and deeper the breath the more effective the cleansing will be. There are many benefit to opening your nostrils to your scent chakras, let's go through them one by one.

Hair Chakra

When assessing the smelth of your hair chakra it is important to note that bad smelling hair has nothing to do with you and everything to do with those around you. Your hair will absorb the their smuth, so be sure to spend your time with people other nostril disciples. If you find people in your life are negatively affecting your hair chakra let them know by saying something like; "Hey man, your negativity is affecting my hair chakra, you should try being more positive and start practising nostril yoga, have you heard about Gary Nostrils?"

If your hair is short you may exchange hair widening breath with another Nostril disciple. You could also try using a patent pending Gary Nostril's enlightenment tube.

Armpit Chakra

If you are particularly pungent in this area it may be due to too much exercise. You should be careful as this could mean you are trying to improve yourself by getting fit. Remember, self-improvement is ego masturbation.

The only thing you need to improve is your nostrils. You can be as lazy and indulgent as you like so long as you focus on improving your nostrils.

Breathing in this chakra is a great way to bring focus back to your nostrils when distraction surrounds you. In a business meeting, on a date or at a party regularly raise your arms and inhale your armpit deeply. This will keep you on the path.

Groin Chakra

Suppressed sexual energy may leak out here as a bad smell. You may need to masturbate more or find more sexual partners to ensure this area smells vibrant and healthy. Be sure to spend at least 20 minutes a day in this pose checking the smelth of your groin chakra.

You may also not be smelling actively enough during sex. Remember to flare your nostrils wide and breathe deeply during sex. Making sure to spend at least 20 minutes inhaling the groin chakra of your partner before penetration.

If you need help with your groin chakra try taking a photo of it and sending it to potential partners on the internet. This will be a clear cry for help that fellow nostril disciples will understand.

Anus Chakra

Many think the anus is always going to be bad smelling. But an enlightened bum smells beautifully. If you find someone claiming to be enlightened, try smelling their anus to discern the smuth of their claims.

Smelling someone's anus to also be a shortcut to ascertaining whether they are telling the truth. If you suspect someone of lying, confront them and refuse to believe them until they let you smell their anus.

As you practice Nostril Yoga you will find the odour of your anus chakra will improve. If you find it is not improving, you may be lying about something or trying to eat healthy food. Beware of diets, like exercise diets are ego driven and will only lead to spiritual ruin.

Feet Chakra

Your feet are the furthest part of your body from your nose. Bad energy may try to hide here to escape your steadily enlightening nose. Bring your widened nostrils as close to your feet as often as you can to make sure no bad energy is residing in them. Insert your nose in between your toes and breathe deeply from every gap.

You will know that you are close to enlightenment when you can walk barefoot and step in anything without developing a bad smell between your toes.

Smelling a person's feet is also a great way to get to know them. The feet chakra will always reveal the smuth of one's smelth. When meeting fellow nostril disciples always greet them by grabbing their right foot and lifting it to one's nose.

Smell heaven

Try to remember, the stronger the smell the more good you are cleansing. Don't be discouraged, you will gain the benefits of a stronger, clearer mind and a purer body, free from negativity. You will shine smuth and smelth wherever you go.

Eventually when you become enlightened you will smell divine. Your sweat will be sweet honey, your snot will be the nougat of the Gods, your saliva with be white wine and your stools will be chocolate cream.

Try test tasting these things regularly to check your progress toward enlightenment.

Cleansing the soul of world

Now that you have practiced cleansing your own soul with your nostrils you can begin to use them to cleanse the world.

When using your breath to cleanse the outside world breath in deeply and as you focus on the out breath, flare your nostrils wide and breathe out in circles. The right nostril clockwise and the left nostril anticlockwise. Imagine spirals coming out of nose as you do this.

Focus your eyes onto the tip of your nose to amplify the power of your breath with your awareness.

You can try this on friends or strangers and judge how open they are to having their soul cleansed.

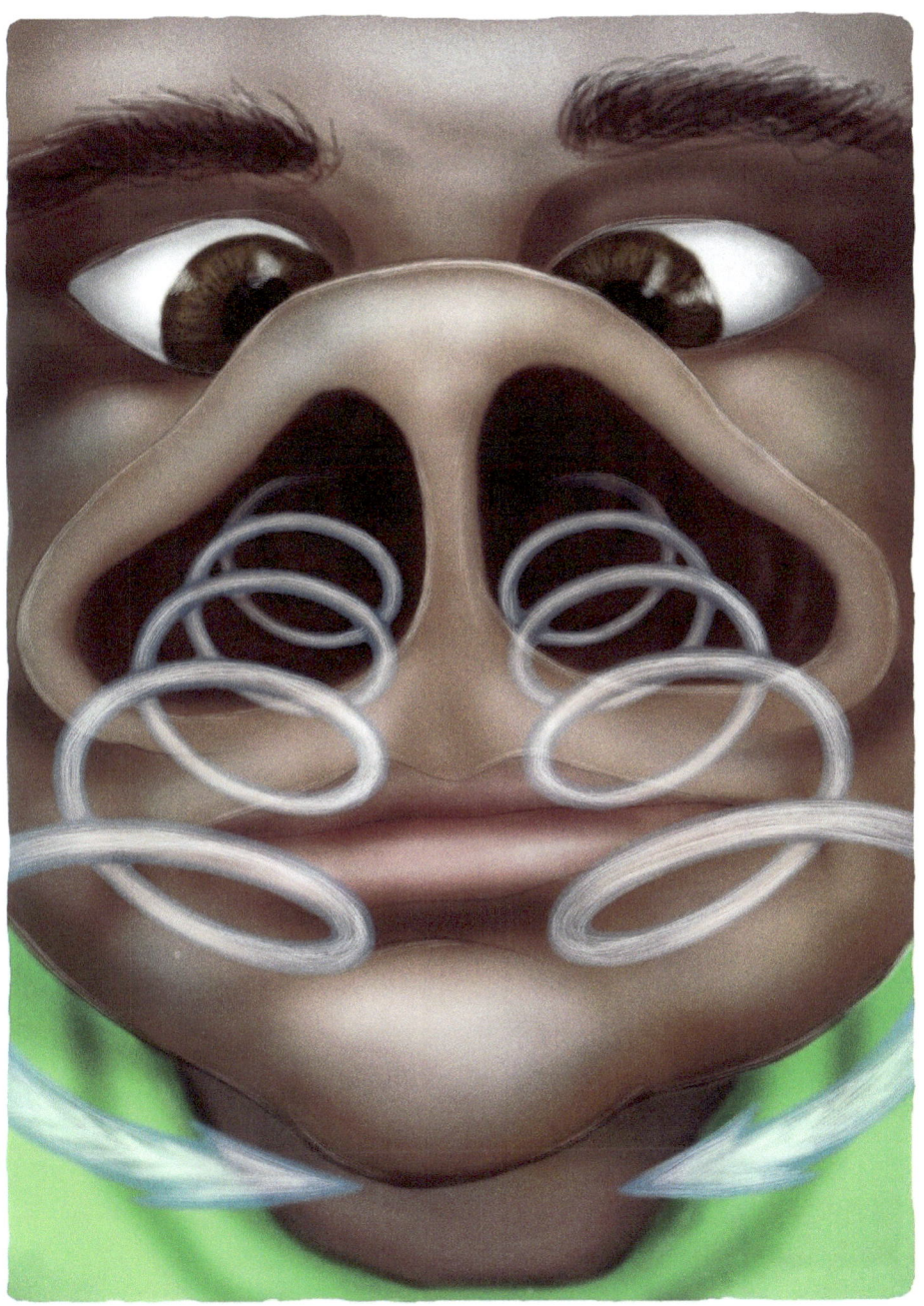

Nostril Cleansing

It is a good practice to regularly cleanse your house with enlightened breath. Be sure to breathe into every area of the house, particularly areas that can store bad smells, like behind the fridge, in the bin or in the toilet.

When you have cleansed your house offer to cleanse your neighbours houses and your place of work. It is important to keep your surroundings as clear of negativity as possible and to strengthen your nostril yoga practice. You may want to do this on a weekly basis or whenever a build-up of negativity has occurred.

If you don't have time you could hire a nostril disciple to do a nostril cleansing for you or if you are in need of work, try advertising yourself as a nostril yogi for hire.

Bad breath

We've all experienced the horror of bad breath. But few of us know its root cause in bad thinking. The more our mind is cluttered and full of judgements the more stinky the mouth. Many people try to hide this with mints, perfumes and excessive teeth brushing, all of which are a lie. As you achieve enlightened breath you do not need to brush to keep a clean mouth, nor do you need to pick your nose to keep it clean. It will be naturally clean as a reflection of their pure mind.

Be watchful of negative thoughts, as they pollute the mind, so they pollute the mouth and nose and then the air. Air pollution itself while it may seem to come from factories, is mostly the result of bad thinking.

I bet she doesn't like sea turtles
He probably stands on snails in his spare time
I bet she hugs pine-apples
He probably eats toast for breakfast...
I bet she drinks tea instead of coffee
Probably doesn't know what a pangolin is...
89107610

Blocking Snot

The nostril will sometimes get clogged, just as in life we sometimes experience setbacks, obstacles or ignorant people. When we get become stuck in life we will inevitably become stuck in our nose. To clear this we must do everything we can to purify our thoughts and clear our life of unwanted possessions and unhelpful people. Blowing one's nose will only treat the symptom. What we must really do is blow all the people and things holding us back from our proverbial nostrils. Each time you get a blocked nose try throwing something away or ending a friendship. Don't worry, as you become more enlightened you will have everything you need and your friends will all be nostril disciples.

Defensive Snot

Sometimes when negativity is trying to get into our body we can form a defensive barrier in the nostril. This is because someone in your life in being negative around you. You can tell the difference between blocking snot and defensive snot by the texture and hardness.

When you discover defensive snot you should immediately find the nearest person and attempt to clear their negativity. Breath in their scent deeply and breath back their purified smell back to them as aggressively as possible, expelling all of the defensive snot back on them. This allows them to take responsibility for their own negativity.

If they are unable to accept responsibility for their own negativity, recommend them this book.

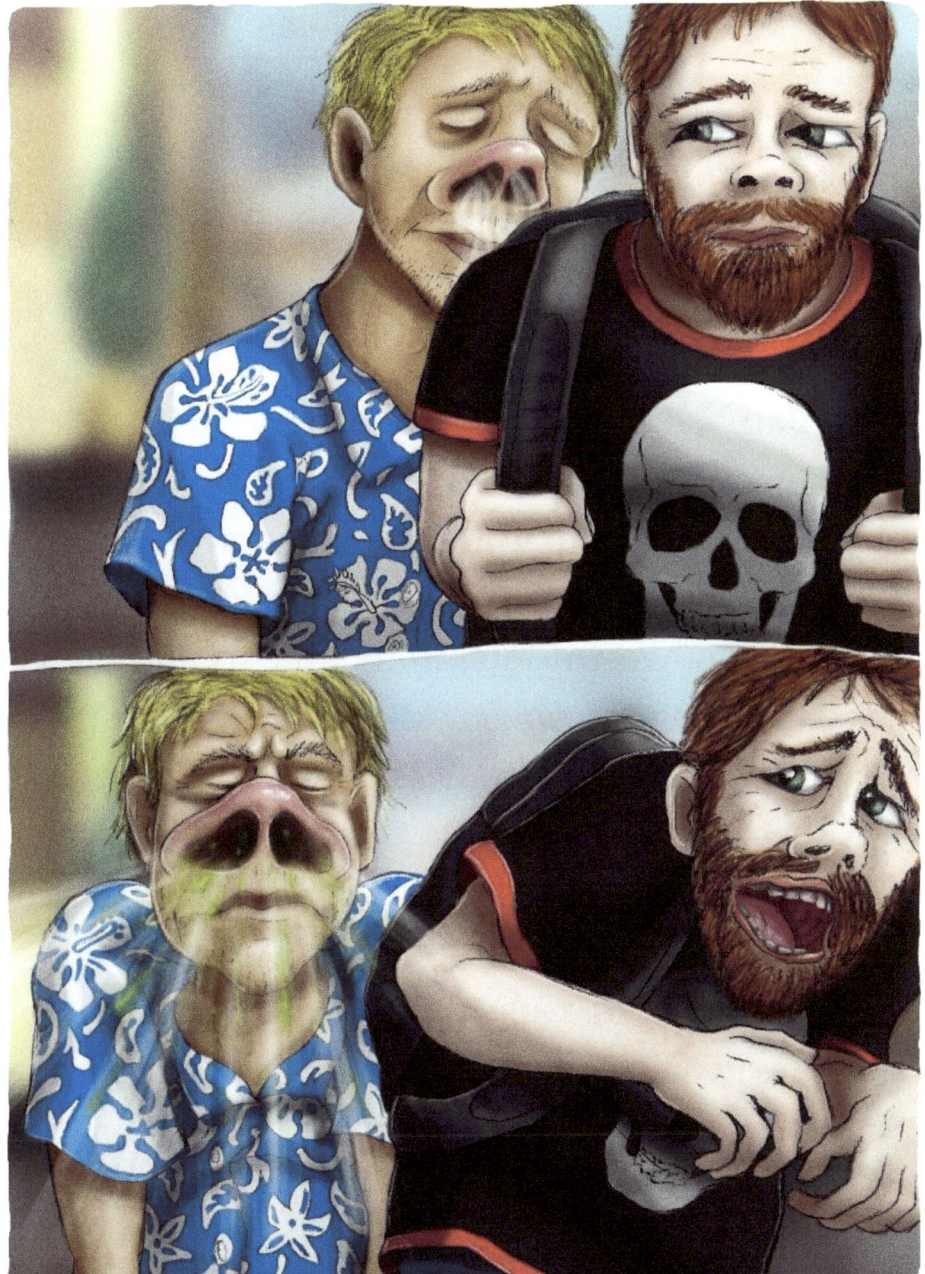

The Breath of Power

To practice the breath of power, breathe in and out through the nose as strongly and loudly as you can. Be sure to flare your nostrils to their maximum.

When breathing this way others will respect and even fear you, but they won't know why. This is a very powerful technique and should be used wisely. Being too powerful can mean other people feel threatened and may react by mocking you to protect themselves. Do not be discouraged, increase your power breath and direct your out breath at those who are laughing.

The power of this breath will push ignorant people away from you and you will find yourself only surrounded by people who understand the true power of nostrils.

Authoritative Breath

Behind every great man is a great woman, but in front of them, are two great nostrils. There were some who were able to achieve greatness without having great breath, but they soon suffered for it. King Harold for example was defeated at the battle of Hastings because his knights didn't follow his orders. This is because he lacked nasal authority, something he could have cultivated by strengthening his nostril muscles. Flexing your nostrils while speaking will lend authority to everything you say. Try flexing them as often as possible, particularly when you are asking people to do things for you.

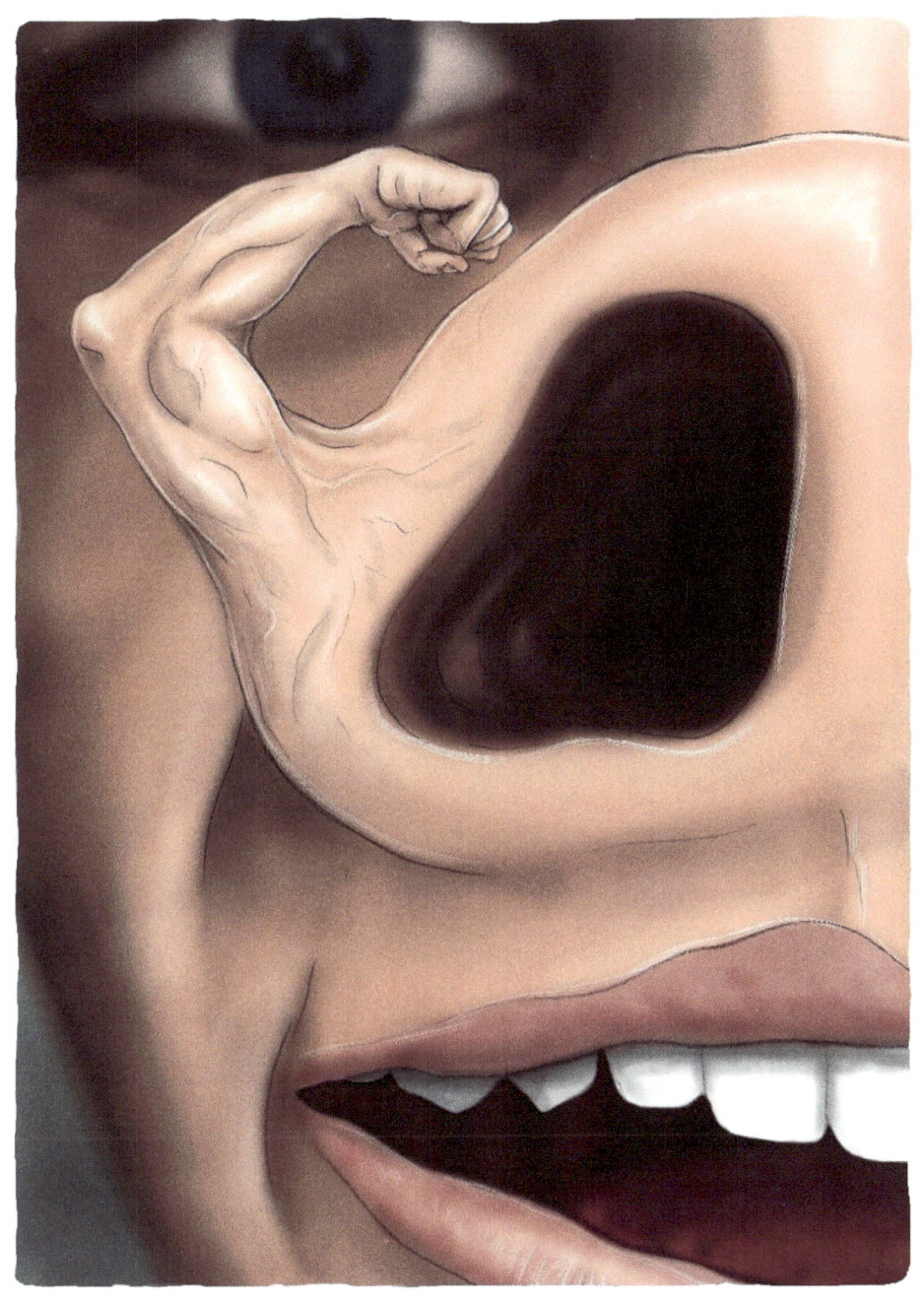

The Breath Strike

You can strike an attacker with the power of your nostrils. This ancient technique predates the Ke ai vocalisation technique and is the forerunner to many qi gong exercises.

To be most effective you must project a strong nasal tone through your nose, making your nostrils vibrate intensely. This sound will confuse and repel anyone who is not full of light and positivity. This is an ideal way to avoid muggings and bar fights.

Learning this technique may take several years and many expensive nostril yoga workshops. Devotion to the cause of Nostril Yoga is essential to developing and channel nostril power.

A World of Enlightened Nostrils

As more nostrils flare to possibility of enlightenment the air on earth will become richer with enlightened breath. Eventually the earth will become so dense with the stench of smelth even those most closed to their nose won't be able to stop from opening a little and experiencing the smuth. Babies will breathe their first breath and immediately have enlightened nostrils.

This dream is possible, and it starts with your nostrils. Open them and a new world awaits...

ABOUT THE AUTHOR

Gary Nostrils is an everyday Aussie bloke from south east Queensland who happens to have enlightened nostrils. He has devoted his life to channelling their wisdom and regularly speaks at festivals, pubs and on street corners.

He is known to his friends as Gazza Nozza or Gaz Noz for short.

You can find him at www.gaznoz.com

www.ingramcontent.com/pod-product-compliance
Lightning Source LLC
Chambersburg PA
CBHW041526090426
42736CB00035B/26